Oases

Jiayin Wang

BookLeaf Publishing

India | USA | UK

Presentation by *BookLeaf Publishing*

Web: www.bookleafpub.com

E-mail: info@bookleafpub.com

ISBN: 9789358316773

First edition 2023

To Dagmar Paulus, who is the best mentor I could ever dream of.

ACKNOWLEDGEMENT

I would like to thank my mother, Lu Zhang, for blessing me with her compassion and insight in life over the years. I am most grateful to my unfailingly loving friends, Ning Xing, Muhan Chen and Weronika Danowska, who have always supported, counselled and encouraged me with their kind words and even kinder actions. I would like to acknowledge with gratitude and love, the generous help of my friend, Jingyao Zhang, without whom this book would not have been possible. My greatest appreciation is for Dagmar Paulus, who has inspired me with her kindness, knowledge and wisdom in literature as well as in life.

TABLE OF CONTENTS

At the Sight of You

The poetry in me dies away.
Streetlamp moons bleeding into the night,
Rain falling endlessly, the world in bleach
Like a black-and-white movie,

Platforms, temporarily quiet,
Smelling of rust and oil; I board
A train of conversations heading to
Or maybe from you,

Following a million directions
Under a cold wintry star and wondering,
With each and every uncertain word,
If you are what I've been looking for.

Farewell

Standing under wavering blue lights and melting
Into the ocean, among paper mache ships and
phantom
Waves, your cheeks warm as though from
drinking,
I catch a glimpse of your rippling hair, your pale
chin hidden
And turning away, the scrawl by an unknown
William:
*The boats are wrecked, some people saved
others*
From the sea. In the days that you are gone
I have come to realise that life is no more
precarious
Than that short-lived dream frozen into reality:

The bluish hue of museum lights
Welling up in your eyes as you turned
To leave, loutish paint crushing ghost ships
Like a parable reversed, and I,
Paralysed by fear and speechless,
Promising that *We will meet again.*

Rain

Rain is an airborne disease,
Seeping into my breath as I waited
Under the roof, creeping, clutching
Clandestinely onto my right lung.
When the earth became a succulent sap,

She joined me under the trickling roof,
Her voice muffled and her face a mist.
Stranded, she gestured subtly
With her smoke: *Do you mind?* And I:
Not at all. In the rain we are but

Drifters; in the rain all fall apart.
Sheltered from the downpour a fire was lit;
She wore black clothing and grey smoke.
An orange speck breathed between her fingers
As its rear end met her lips. The sky

Was suspended far above, an inaudible,
Watery slab of blue. Rain makes everything
A laceration; rain makes everything
A healing bruise. We waited in silence
As a thousand silvery daggers plunged down

From the impalpable blue. *Enjoy the rain,*

She finally said, leaving her cigarette burning.
The sky was a highway overhung,
Monotonous, forlorn and abstractly vast,
Waiting to dry under an invisible moon.

When the sound of the rain died out,
For a moment I inhaled faultless air.
Her smoke had long evanesced,
But there lived still its misty ghost
Which, hovering like the ghost of the rain,

Would never let go. The rain had belonged
To both of us. When she left, the rain was mine.

Highland Seas

I stand by the sea and think:
What a glorious graveyard.

The dead ship sails in waves
Softer than a mother's touch,
Until its hull peels away and its keel
Becomes ridges of steel, a vertebra
In the seabed's massive skeleton.

The dead bird flies faster
Than a train of thought, over fields
Of coral and swamps of kelp,
Into clear waters undisturbed
By the rippling morning light.

The dead poet sings with a voice
As slick as pebble and as white as sand,
Alive and ablaze, wavering
Between the leaves of algae or
Carried on the fins of fish.

One day I too will trespass
That land of mead and song.
I will breathe through my fingertips
And dream when days are long.

House Party

It never fails to alarm me:
How warm a place it is, clouded with
Steamy joy and booming indie music
Under swimming blue lights,

How it coaxes me into forgetfulness,
That illusory safety promising
To last forever like a ticking watch,
A fractured vow,

Yet just as I begin to lean against
Cotton-candy walls, there comes
The setting of the sun; birds with
Quiet tongues; a late bell chiming.

September Dream

Like a supernova you descended
Upon my dream, in a white trench coat
That flapped in the autumnal wind like wings,
Joking to make me laugh the night I understood
What we were would always tear us apart.

In hindsight I read
With alarming transparency
That look of grief in your eyes, of knowing
How we would lose each other to a dim-lit
future
Swaying in speech, of homeless birds and
mountains,
Someone's porch forlorn with wind chimes,
Mute and full of tears.

I lost your cherry blossom spoon
Before realising what we had was love.

Many a time I imagined holding your hand,
And made you promise with a cloud-draped
heart
We would never drift apart. You gazed at me
calmly
With a kindness most often seen in a mother's
eyes

As her son weeps *What would I do if you die?*
And she croons, *I won't,* stroking his cheek,
Knowing he will keep on living.

False Alarm

1

A man with long arms and a broken guitar came to me
With love on sale. *Who did you sell it to?* His cart was
Almost empty. *He who lived in a fishbone. She who sang*
To groves. He whose lobelia was dying. She whose
Grief was long. He, with eyes like sunset. She, with clasped
Hands. He who painted nothing. She who had no time.

2

A girl who wore mud on her cheek asked me to choose
Between a pen and a rose. *Tell me more*, I said.
The pen has no present and the rose has no past.
The pen dries, as it should. The rose withers, as it should.
They both drink from glasses not yet broken. They both are
One and the same.

3

A fox in the desert came and went. The dunes were
Harsh and golden.

4

A bad dancer chose the rose. *I would have picked the pen*
If writing felt less like drowning, filling blanks with blanks.
A pilot chose the rose. *My limestone heart is porous.*
A fox stopped to lick a grain of sand off the bottom of his paw.

5

You should love, said the man with the guitar, *it makes life*
Less hazardous. I gave him a penny, asked him what life was.
Old records, he said. *Refusing to be carried downstream.*
Ten thousand nights of almost dying.

6

Let me have love, I said. *I sleep in a fishbone, with long*
And shadowy grief. I drink ink, then water. I crash planes and

*Step on leather shoes. I am sloshed with sand. I
give you my pen*
For a fistful of love. His cart was empty. A fox
came and said,
*Come back when the price tag falls. You are
nothing but lonely.*

Blur

You dare not let yourself drown
In the infinitely corruptive sea of anticipation
Until early July, that effervescent afternoon
When you board the clanking train and
The world's a riot, you gasp to inhale
Coloured air and everything that comes after.

With every step you take, you hear
A thousand echoing others, a thousand hearts,
Booming and swelling, slippery with sweat and
joy,
Gripping you tight and pulling you into
A thousand swirling seas. On both sides of the
road
There are matte rainbows and a sign that reads
All of Blur's Rubbish.

When you arrive there's no telling which is
louder,
Your pulse or the drums. The sun is malignant,
The faceless crowd without a voice
Squirmy and squeaky. You hold on to your
jacket
As if your life depends on it, and hope that it
soon begins,
That clouds are made of soot or gullies.

Then with a sudden blast the stadium roars
And you hear your heart drop, drop, drop,
Until caught by a beat, a skip, a white noise in
time,
Which is when you start breathing again.
The morningtide retreats, engulfing you
With its crimson evening flood, endless strings
Strummed by countless fingers.

And for a moment you are blinded
By the screams, you drink in the electric air
As if it were a mere whisper, an ocean overhung.
For a moment the world is swollen with sound,
Like a prehistoric wound
Opening.

For a moment two moons shine above and you
forget,
Letting your soul drift away as if to cheat out of
life
The permission never to return.
For a moment you are drunk with oxygen,
With one voice or ten thousand more on stage,
And in trying to recover your own
You are drowned out by floodlights.

For a moment you become nothing,
Transparent enough for the world to see through.

For a moment there is an explosion of stars,
Of raging waters and rising tides, and you feel
safe
Without thinking, because any joy must be idle
And you forget with content.

For a moment there is only an eternal pause,
No men or women, no peace or war;
For a moment you recognise life itself,
Furious and in anguish, sung by voices
Splitting and in tears. For a moment
You hear the swan song before the presage,
The birchwood before the waves.

For a moment the world is a nighttime dovecote,
And then there was light,
And then there was nothing.

1996

Nostalgia is a fiction if instead of memory you have
Only a second-hand CD with its crust flaking,
Blurring echoing rains of fireworks into a mawkish
Melancholy, erasing all expressions from
That bustling crowd younger than youth itself

Until all you're left with is an aftertaste of ecstacy,
A grand narrative profoundly concluded, an open field
Littered with half-empty plastic cups of beer still sweating
Under a moon unseen, a dapper fellow perched on a branch
And a throng of voices underneath, departing and booming

Hey you! Up in a tree, you wanna be me? Now the tape
Rewinds and you wonder how anyone could steal from this life
Time you haven't spent and risks you haven't taken,

How you crave the unreachable with a wild and tongueless
Ache, chasing your own tail until finally you see

In your mind's eye that crazed and passionate end,
Approaching infinitely a paling brilliance, a dying of the
Centurial sun, when roads were thin and joy impendent,
With an unfailing bravado of impromptu trips and alternative
Rock, when the guidebook to life was a map of poetic

Imprecision, when the world was raw and unfiltered, faithfully
Evanescent in reckless, exuberant eyes. You hit play and he
Resurfaces from a summertime uproar, crying
Are you madferit?
Hugging your knees, you sit homeward and unblinking,
Briefly permanent, mildly out of time.

Sold-out

Nothing is ever as simple as itself. Outrunning
My capriciousness, I asked in a rapture,
Where will this journey lead me? Nowhere, I
knew it
Already. You squint under a late summer sun
and see
There is no finish line, no track, no audience.
Your heart leaps up roguishly but your mind sits
still
Until you start to exhale wind which will be as
dead
As air when you stop running. All destinations
are
A mirage, I know it already. But still I wonder:
What am I running from? Every journey must
end
Somewhere. *The starvation of your soul,* I lie,
Possibly. If I had one, I would ask for clemency
-

What does it mean to have lived? My soul, the
living
Wind, replies: *You know it already, when you
ran*
*Two miles, maybe three, to a box office with no
tickets*

Left. To be a fox and wander. To be Sisyphus.
To aim at the empty, breathe life into air.

Each Man Kills the Thing He Loves

Sunless, you refuse to turn away but gaze on
As the final splash dies out under the docks, dumbfounded
By an unspeakable absence, a heavenly *beyond*
Enclosed within a set of ribs that feels like
Anyone's but yours. From

The hungry glare of that child of Gehenna you liberate
Yourself. From his cheeky sprawl, ungainly walk,
His unearthly and sultry leer that always sent you reeling,
Like sniffing glue but more confessional, almost undying,
Almost worth dying *for.* He lived

In bitten apples, in the silent studying eyes of goats,
Had a soul of crossed swords, a mind endlessly adrift
With ecstasy, vomited into clouds and forbade
The pushing of brakes. You heard running streams

And drank his voice like cider,

Grieving with no words, reeking of a tear too late
Or a heart too heavy. There is no greater sin than tolerance
For a word unspoken, a balance restored, a wrong forgiven.
You drove head-on towards an open cliff, the sea of glass unmoving
Until that quiet splash, when his lungs soak up water
And yours air,

And you gaze on, as if facing Tartarus,
Engulfed by a murderous rebirth or a homecoming,
Your arms open and full of wind, your eyes
Not yet calm but drying,
As if by denying love you may conquer
Everything.

Manchester

1

Arriving cripples me with proximity:
The closer I come, the greater my fears
For the loss of a reason
For this dream not to come true.

2

I see your face on lost ungraffitied walls.
I hear your voice wherever.

3

When I thought of your city
I imagined homecoming. I imagined
Dimming lights, garrets with bleary windows,
Snow falling, you falling asleep. As a child
You had ethereal eyes. As a child
You were seen smiling.

4

I dislike that the city is large enough
For you to speak and I not to hear it.

5

Your city is full of echoes, made of ochre
And glass, clouds hanging lower
Than melancholia. I am suspended in

Midair. Cold spires and furling flags,
Nothing like your brother and everything
Like you. Your draughty heart feels
This close to healing.

6
The love you never speak of is as foreign
As the city itself, a permanent crack in my
Window, slanted but breathing.
I fail to picture you in birdcalls,
In a wordless aching of the soul, smoking
With one bare foot on your stereo, a golden
Friday
Of skin and salt, eyes closed,
Seeing everything. In its midsummer
Solitude your city says: *Life is less hollow*
When you sleep without dreams.

On the Train

1

Your phantom grip on me, though slackening
over time,
Outlives all prescience of grief, hidden in flashes
of green
And profusely in retreat. We have only so many
chances
To be briefly out of time.

2

I sit on a train not facing you to cancel out my
dread
In vain. Gazing on and seeing nothing,
approaching but
Never arriving at that inmaterial place which I,
once
Drenched in tears, called home.

3

I clutch in my palms like the Bible those words
you wrote,
My soul huddled underneath, foreign and
cerulean,
Feverishly aglow. Elation feels like the tide
churning;
I wish for your moon to change its course.

4

At the point of no return I find myself willing to
sacrifice
Any transient proximity to be spared from
comprehending
With unforgiving clarity the loutishness of our
distance
Ever present and diminishing - I am the tide,
perhaps.

To Him In The White Jumper, Smoking

I see you there, an eternal fiction,
With a lifted chin and sunglassed eyes,
Reaching your hand up high
As if holding a pistol in a race match,
Or clutching someone's soul
Waiting to be buried by ashes.

One last puff and be done with it;
Watch the whole world crumble as they
Scream your name, twelve thousand hearts
In your hands, your fingers closing in
Around what is otherwise known as
A burnt-out fire, an emptiness,
A universal boredom.

On the Road

Did you know of teary-eyed silence,
Of words unspoken, of cities deserted
And clouds overhung like you now do?
By a grove off the highway

You plot a slumber for your car:
Headlights turned off, engine idling,
Filled with swooning reverie and
Breathless; very much asleep,

Cradled in an air of whiskey.
You smell blatant cheap leather,
Sunset shrouding the distant hills;
The whole world set ablaze above you,

Ignorant, love thirsty, gasping for air.
On the road there is no past or future;
It is always you, always him, always now.
You know you would rather die than

Loosen your grasp on his troubled heart
Brimming with pain. The dawn is red
And his rains are falling; but how vile
A world he is! Turbulent are his oceans,

Tempestuous his trees. You have before you

A thousand other gods, their eyes more virtuous
And their touch more sweet; yet still
You lean into him, that torpid stupor,

That faceless dream. It is when the rain stops
That you realise *we are what we love.*
You are him. Hopefully, he will love you
Before you bury him.

Graffiti

1

Blank canvas is a birthright, so the man believes. The man paints over a wall of paintings for a white wall of his own. This is how you create a vacuum, or art. How different can they be? Art is the narration of nothing.

2

The man has a bland heart which is not a heart but an enclosed empty, sucking on air and desperate to be full. Can a white wall satisfy the hunger of a cavity sinking? On Saturday nights, maybe.

3

The world is too small for his wall, so the man carries it on his shoulder, blocking out traffic and not hearing honks. The man is not deaf, but can be when it suits him. All artists are deaf but not mute: the key to being heard, invincible.

4

The man paints a wall over and sweeps out the lane. White is all-conquering, has the lifespan of a government, is all the zeros in maths, the rim of a dead dog's eye, the overlayering of almost-transparency. The man lets a white wall stand in the middle, watches other colours retreat in contempt. The place becomes nowhere, a cavity taken out of his chest and into the world, expanding.

5

The man paves slabs of red paint on the white wall, which is a metaphor for nothing except words, but only good words have meaning. Saturday nears its end. The sky retreats. No one can make sense of a metaphor with a vacuum of a heart.

6

Colours return after sunrise, maybe.

7

The man bears a white wall on his shoulder. Hangs it on the empty from and of his heart.

Mother

Every once in a while I am presented
With a kindness so infinite in depth
And selfless in nature that it would be
A worry to receive and a sin to refuse.
It is from moments like this that I realise,
With a sadness universally unnamed,
The truth in life's attic: to be burdened
By love's ultimate self, that taxing
Grandeur, that immaculate luxury,
Like a deaf bell-ringer at midnight or
A weightless, wingless bird, trudging
Through slush, leaving no claw marks.

Father's Photo

An immense premonition of freedom in life,
More wintry and biting than late autumn brooks,
Weighed down her soul with slackening
shoulders
As she gazed, with silent iniquity, at the face
Of the man whom her mother allegedly loved,
Whom she could never recognise. He looked
Nondescript - a bad copy of the ghost she used
to
Dream and brag unabashedly about; he looked
Like nothing she knew. In that intense moment
Of self-inflicted pain, she inquired with some
Disappointment: *Who are you, sad rootless
child?*
And realised: *Mother is one's only tie to this
Homeless world.* Seized by an unyielding joy
She gazed on, if only for him to be more foreign;
The voice of a savage goddess called, so far
away
Like an albatross, for her to feel in its entirety
The breaking of that fictional chain, the
extraction
Of the given rib, a confrontation that frightens
before
It liberates, until she was free to descend,
weightless

Into an unnamed void of rebellious ecstasy,
A shade of grey between blood and oblivion,
To take a newborn breath, her heart pounding
With the fearful silence of a survival
unaccounted for,
As one attempts death by hanging in a
snow-capped forest
With the discretion of a martyr, only for the
branch to
Snap.

Come, Edmund, to the Sea

You, lonely poet of the sea: you are the son
Of tragedy. Before knowing you I have met you
A thousand times in my dreamless sleep,
Until you woke me up, your breath tasting like
liquor,
Inviting me to a walk by the nighttime shore.
The moon, Edmund, was kind and milky,
Seaweeds drifting in shallow cyan waves.
I looked at you and saw: a fish born without
gills,
A bird without wings. Come with me, Edmund,
To the life-giving, life-wrecking sea.
When the moon wanes and the tide rises,
When the fog lifts its gauze and draws you in,
Let those waves loom over the saturated night,
And let that which we love the most
Become the death of us.

Questions for Edmund

Will you remember dying young,
When the firmament darkens
And subsides into the boiling sea?
Will you remember how, with your brow
Gently raised and your eyes narrowed
In a smile, you discovered the one
Secret: that the world is at its end, that
Religion is a fraud, that life is
Contagious and afflicted by default?
Will you remember lifting, lifting the veil,
And finding nothing underneath?
Will you remember letting a sigh
Escape your cold red mouth,
As tuberculosis ravaged through your
Battered veins, leaving nothing behind
But dying poetry?

Writing Poetry Is:

Reminiscence. The digging of graves before any news of death,
A living funeral, not to mourn but to remember, to carve out
An immortal something, as grand, fierce and overwhelming
As waves at an undated beach, to leave it behind for nameless visitors.
Observance through the eyes of a stag, albeit temporarily;
Then: the whiskers of a tiger, the windswept tail of a diving gull.

Carrying this rock-hard feeling in your stomach: that you and your poem
Are the same poles of two magnets; that your straining fingertips might,
With a desperate enough reach, brush over what is infinitely yours -
That brief and blessed *click* - before it slips from your grasp,
The ghostly remnant of an existence once so concrete, so faithfully
Built out of words: the most indestructible of all deathless things.

www.ingramcontent.com/pod-product-compliance
Lightning Source LLC
La Vergne TN
LVHW010922200726
843509LV00013B/2034